Phonic Rhyme Time

Phonic Rhyme Time

First edition published by
The Robinswood Press 1993

© Mary Nash-Wortham 1993

Design and illustrations by Alison Shepherd

Printed by Wynstones Press

The Robinswood Press
Stourbridge England
DY8 3XY

ISBN 1 869981 47 2

CONTENTS

FOREWORD

In a world said to be growing ever smaller, the ability to communicate clearly and precisely becomes increasingly important. Methods of fast, easy communication proliferate, and will become increasingly sophisticated as the technological revolution continues. While this in itself is exciting, all these developments will flounder unless we build solid foundations. Those foundations are the basics - language and speech.

Speech is itself a development of the most primary instinct of the human child - making one's feelings known. The new-born baby will express its discomfort by crying and screaming. Quickly, though, children discover more subtle and precise ways of communicating their perceptions, leading to the development of speech and language skills.

Clear speech and communication skills are not just a basic human instinct. They are a basic human right. It is impossible to pay too much attention to developing sympathy for, and knowledge of, the basic sounds of language. Not only does this make children aware of the potential richness and flexibility of the spoken word, but has an important 'spin-off' effect on the development of literacy.

As Principal of Examinations at the London Academy of Music and Dramatic Art, my initial interest in Phonic Rhyme Time was as a teaching aid for Speech and Drama teachers dealing with students with particular areas of difficulty in pronunciation, breath control and voice production. Both children and adults find that rhymes act as tremendous mnemonics for repeated practice in a particular area. It is no accident that the earliest literature of every culture was fixed in a form of verse, often heavily rhymed, to aid oral transmission from one generation to another. This collection of intelligent rhymes for each sound - and one in which the concentration of the sound in each rhyme is so strong - is an invaluable tool for every teacher and student. Certainly, some of this ground has been covered in other publications, but never, in my experience, as precisely as by Mary Nash-Wortham in Phonic Rhyme Time. There is nothing worse, as a teacher, than using a rhyme to develop a particular sound, only to find that the rhyme itself contains too many other sounds, some close to the one being developed - the result is confusion in the student's mind and, all too often, failure of the original intention.

I would heartily recommend this book to all teachers of Speech and Drama as a precise and definitive workbook for the development of clear speech. But there is a great deal more to it than that, with applications across a large number of fields. Research has proved definitely that pre-reading children benefit enormously from being introduced to the ideas of rhyme, alliteration and assonance. Children exposed to phonics and sound-categorisation early in their education have, time and again, developed reading skills much more quickly and effectively than those children who have not. Spelling, too, is an area in which spectacular results can be seen - and spelling is an essential tool for clear written communication.

Clearly, this research also has major implications for those children and adults who have had difficulties with literacy and speech under the traditional system of teaching. One of the joys of phonics is that it is never too late to start exploring them. Adults with literacy or speech problems often feel intimidated not only at admitting their problem, but at starting with what feel like 'baby-ish' texts. Phonics cut through these problems, as they are a means of educating 'from a different angle'. This means that teaching can be varied from person to person, at a level appropriate to their age and intellectual capacity. Teaching through and with phonics can be an exciting journey of discovery even for those who have come to feel that there is no way forward for them.

There is always a way forward. There is always more to learn, whatever one's age or position in life. I have found Phonic Rhyme Time enormously illuminating and thought-provoking. I commend it to you without reservation.

Shaun McKenna - Principal of Examinations - The London Academy of Music and Dramatic Art.

INTRODUCTION

'Phonics' are back in focus. Modern research shows that the study of single vocal sounds - known as phonics - and the use of rhymes help children to understand and learn the basic principles of speech, and achieve reading and spelling accuracy.

Everyone interested in the development of communication needs to understand the process of actual oral sound production. From this knowledge we can help to build the individual's own concept and feel for language. There are some basic functions which must be in use if the technical aspects of speech are to be achieved. These are:-

Breath Control	- its quantity and force.
Voice	- rapid vibrations of the vocal cords to create sound waves.
Resonance and Projection	- the quality of sound produced and carried.
Tongue and Lips	- synchronous, rapid, active movements.
Soft Palate and Jaw Movements	- physical control.
Pronunciation	- actual formation of consonants and vowels.
Phrasing	- linking of words together to make sense.
Pitch, Tone and Stress	- to create a flow of words with meaning and interest.
Rhythm and Pace	- to provide continuity and feeling.

All these areas are normally developed without real awareness of the process involved. Experience and usage extend the child's own level of ability to communicate effectively. Normally, the feel for sounds in the mouth is developed by the young baby as it coos and babbles its way through an experimental period before embarking on a whole first word.

First words develop into little songs and nursery rhymes; the sense of rhythm and timing is well established in the first few years of life. The co-ordinated development between sound and symbol begins to take place quite naturally with the introduction of activities involving hand and eye co-ordination including touch, feel, and active, purposeful movements. These may include rolling pastry, shaping with Plasticine and scribbling or daubing splashes of paint which introduce the basic feeling for lines and curves of letter shapes.

Language inter-relates between speaking, reading and writing. Every word is made up of consonants with at least one vowel with its own form or shape. In speech, the position of the lips, tongue, jaw and soft palate create the sound, either with 'voice' when the vocal cords vibrate, or 'voiceless' when just force of air flows through the open cords and against the articulators. Rapid movements produce synchronized single sound links which build into the desired word. Those words, strung together, build sentences. Within sentences, the personal framework of communication is built through the use of new dimensions of vocabulary - or the knowledge and choice of meaningful words - and the even more complex areas of syntax or grammar.

This brief summary explores the 'expressive' or heard side of speech. On the other side is the listener who is receiving the words as 'receptive' language. For the whole expressive and receptive interchange to work effectively through the neurological pathways of the brain, reception for speech must be intact and there must be normal hearing ability. However, for as many as one in four children, the process does not just happen as a matter of course. Practice has to be introduced as a support to help the desired development and fend off frustration in the child.

Phonic Rhyme Time gives immediate access to an English rhyme, jingle, or phrase, with strong alliteration or assonance, for every single indexed consonant, consonant blend and vowel variation found in words, at the initial (or beginning-), the medial (or middle-) and the final (or end-of-word) positions.

The selected sound can be practised with concentration, as a speech rhyme, as reading and even as a rhyme for dictation to gain spelling confidence. This multi-sensory approach is recommended in research and in practice. This promotes the senses to maximum advantage, using the ears to hear the sound, the eyes to link the written symbol with the spoken and heard sound, while gaining the feel of the sound in the mouth by its very repetition. There are many ways of extending this theme to suit the particular needs of the individual or group.

Generally, Phonic Rhyme Time will be used for specific target practice, aiming to build blocks of sound sequences and extend vocabulary. The rhymes are meant to be a useful resource tool, and as such can be a supplement to the host of wonderful children's poetry books that are readily available in book shops. A selection of favourites are listed as an appendix at the end of this book together with some useful publications on speech and language.

The verses are purely functional. They are intended as fun examples rather than works of art. All have been used with, or developed by, children and adults over the years in our attempts to lift the fog of confusion and doubt which often surrounds the amazing human sound system. Just a few classic masterpieces of poetry are included to give fine examples of expressive clarity and rhythm whilst still keeping phonic sound as the main theme. The intended age range is wide. The simple rhymes for younger or less advanced pupils are given first, then some quite challenging vocabulary is linked with the more complex sound groups for older or more advanced students, including those learning English as a foreign language.

Mary Nash-Wortham M.C.S.L.T.   1993

ACKNOWLEDGEMENTS

The Book includes some copyright poems and I thank the publishers and authors for kindly granting permission to use them. Acknowledgement is made under the poem where it occurs in the text. I would also like to thank everyone directly or indirectly, young or old, who has been or is involved in the evolution and production of the manuscript and its illustrations. Without their enthusiasm, imagination and encouragement Phonic Rhyme Time would not have been completed. We welcome constructive additions, observations and comments for future editions. (MNW)

SPEECH SOUNDS AND THEIR CREATION

Speech sounds are made with a flow of expelled air passing between the vocal cords. If the cords vibrate there is 'voiced' sound, otherwise 'voiceless' air passes up into the mouth where the soft palate, tongue and lips all move in rapid synchronisation to produce a co-ordinated flow of sounds, or 'phonemes', which are normally heard as meaningful speech and language.

Every word we say has to have a vowel sound in it. There are over twenty vowel sounds and they all need variable open mouth and particular tongue and lip shaping to give each voiced vowel its correct quality. Plenty of practice sentences are given in this book to help say and listen to the differences. Regional accents and dialects increase the variety of sounds, especially vowels - emphasis can change without reducing clarity. 'Good' speech depends on clarity rather than any 'accent'.

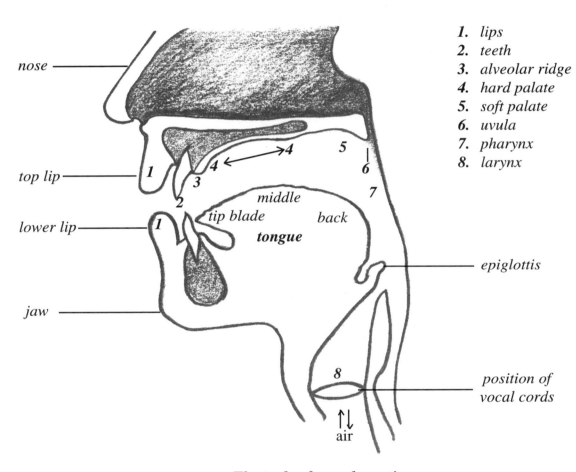

1. lips
2. teeth
3. alveolar ridge
4. hard palate
5. soft palate
6. uvula
7. pharynx
8. larynx

The tools of sound creation

Indistinct speech needs analysing: is the pace incorrect, the articulation weak, or even defective? Maybe there are omitted sounds or even substitutions, when one sound is used instead of another. With careful observation and deduction, the cause of indistinct speech may be isolated. It may then be overcome with a little helpful encouragement on how to listen to and repeat the sounds and then build them into rhymes followed by sentences or a short story.

There must never be any 'pressure' put on a child who is struggling to speak. Any real defects should be looked into by a specialist speech and language therapist without delay. The longer a defect persists the harder it is to change as it can become an established habit factor, or maybe part of a more serious overall problem.

8

However, there are many occasions when the help required to overcome 'slow to get going' or 'slow to catch on' may be given quite naturally in the classroom setting. A friendly, relaxed approach can have a happy outcome as part of the normal lesson. Parents often enjoy helping to 'back up' the progress with home practice. They can give encouragement with the association of the heard, seen and spoken sound, using some of the abundant educational ideas - from good old-fashioned 'I Spy' to modern board and computer games. As long as the activities are enjoyable, the learning process will be taking place, consolidating and developing, although sometimes it can seem to take a long time. Discouragement or disinterest must be avoided, or resolved with a different approach.

'Phonics' teaching does take time, planning and patience, but correctly linked into speech, reading and spelling, it will help youngsters to gain understanding and confidence in English as their language.

CATEGORIES OF PHONIC SOUNDS

Sound Category	Voiceless	Voiced	Sound Creation
Plosives	p	b	*Lips together, briefly.*
	t	d	*Tongue tip on alveolar ridge, briefly.*
	c, k	g	*Back of tongue against soft palate, briefly.*
Fricatives	f	v	*Top teeth lightly on bottom lip.*
	th	th	*Tongue tip between teeth, gently.*
	s	z	*Tongue and alveolar ridge close, teeth very close.*
	sh	zh	*Tongue edges and upper side teeth very close.*
	h		*Open mouth and blow.*
Affricates	ch	j	*Tongue against alveolar ridge, slow release.*
Lateral Non-fricative		l	*Tongue tip touching centre of alveolar ridge.*
Semi-vowels		w	*Rounded lips.*
		y	*Mouth slightly open, lips back.*
Frictionless Continuant		r	*Tongue tip raised behind alveolar ridge, not touching it.*
Nasal		m	*Lips together, hold. Sound down nose.*
		n	*Tongue tip up, hold. Sound down nose.*
		ng	*Back of tongue up, hold. Sound down nose.*

PHONIC RHYME CHART

Allow a few minutes to feel, in your own mouth, how single sounds vary in their position - try /p/ then /g/. Once you have experimented with making sounds, it will be easier to use the following chart to find a particular sound and therefore a corresponding rhyme. The chart is arranged so that each sound category (for example, plosives) shows both the position of the sound within the word - initial, medial, or final - and for each position a group of sounds which runs from the front of the mouth to the back.

Position:	Initial	Medial	Final	Page
Plosives	/p/ /pl/ /pr/	/p/ /pl/ /pr/	/p/ /mp/ /lp/ /rp/	12-14
	/b/ /bl/ /br/	/b/ /bl/ /br/	/b/ /lb/ /rb/	15-18
	/t/ /tr/ /tw/	/t/ /tr/ /tw/	/t/ /rt/ /lt/ /ft/	19-22
	/d/ /dr/ /dw/	/d/ /dr/ /dl/	/d/ /ld/ /rd/	23-25
	/c/ /k/ /cl/ /cr/ /qu/	/c/ /k/ /cl/ /cr/ /qu/	/ck/ /k/ /lk/ /rk/	26-30
	/g/ /gl/ /gr/	/g/ /gr/	/g/	31-33
Fricatives	/f/ /fl/ /fr/	/f/ /fl/ /fr/	/f/ /lf/ /rf/	34-37
	/v/	/v/	/v/ /lv/	38-39
	/th/ /thr/	/th/	/th/	40-42
	/s/ /sp/ /st/ /sc/	/s/ /sp/ /st/ /sc/	/ss/ /sp/ /st/ /sk/	43-49
	/scr/ /sm/ /sn/ /sl/			49-50
	/sw/ /spr/ /str/ /squ/ / spl/			50-52
	/z/	/z/	/z/	53-54
	/sh/ /shr/	/sh/	/sh/	55-56
	/h/	/h/		57
Affricates	/ch/	/ch/	/ch/	58
	/j/	/j/	/j/	59
Lateral Non-fricatives	/l/	/l/	/l/	60-61
			/pl/ /bl/ /tl/ /dl/ /cl/	
			/gl/ /fl/ /sl/ /zl/	62-64
Semi-vowels	/w/ /wh/	/w/	/w/	65-66
	/y/			67
Frictionless Continuant	/r/	/r/	/r/	68
Nasal	/m/ /n/	/m/ /n/ /ng/	/m/ /n/ /shn/ /ng/	69-72
Vowels	Pure short: /a/ /e/ /i/ /o/ /u/ /oo/ /er/			73-74
	long: /ee/ /ah/ /aw/ /oo/ /er/			74-75
	Diphthongs: /ay/ /oh/ /I/ /ow/ /oi/ /eer/ /air/ /ure/ /ew/			75-77
	Triphthongs: /ire/ /our/			77

INDEX TO PHONIC RHYMES IN ALPHABETICAL ORDER

FURTHER READING

Since Phonic Rhyme Time has been designed for wide usage by parents as well as teachers and therapists, many of whom will not be familiar with 'Phonetics', the standardised International Phonetic Symbols have been avoided. Further reading is listed in the appendix for those interested in developing greater understanding in this area.

Pens poised,
Pencils pointed,
Pass paper,
Picture perfect.

Pitter patter, pitter patter,
Who can hear the rain?
Pitter patter, pitter patter,
On the window pane.

Winifred Kingdon-Ward

/p/ medial position

Offer a puppy a slipper -
Upper part soon disappears,
Offer a puppy some supper
Puppy will not disappoint, then -
Happily into slumber he topples.

/p/ final position

Cup up, tip up, mop up.
Hop up, run up, sit up.

/mp/ final position

Romp and jump.
What a bump!
A big lump,
Like a hump,
Has come up on my rump!

/pl/ initial position

'Planes plague,
Planks plonk,
Plates are platters,
Plump plums give pleasure.

/pl/ medial position
The sound /pl/ at ends of words comes under the /l/ group.

Supply the pen and paper
Apply some lines of news
Employ a stamp to send it,
Now wait for the reply!

/lp/ final position

Up an Alp

Help, help!
Avalanche on the Alp.
I'm going to be pulp.
Yelp, yelp!
Dog finds me from that faint 'Help'
Gulp, gulp!
What a relief on the Alp.

/pr/ initial position

Proud ponies prance prettily.

Pretty but practical,
Practical and praiseworthy,
Praiseworthy, so precious,
Precious the prayer,
Prayer in private,
Private but prized,
Prized beyond price.

/pr/ medial position

Approve the idea.
Improve the content.
Reproduce the image.
Reprove the bad.
Reprimand the naughty.
Reprieve the guilty.

/rp/ final position
/r/ may be heard, or blend into vowel.

Slurp, slurp,
Burp, burp!

14

Bees buzz,
Boats bob,
Babies bawl,
Buds burst,
Big bands boom
BANG, BANG, BANG.

Bubble, bubble, bubble,
Says the kettle.
Bubble, bubble, bubble,
Says the pot.
Bubble, bubble, bubble,
We are very hot!

Traditional

The 'Bitter Butter' rhyme (page19) is also good practice for /b/ initial position.

Robber runs.
Cupboard bare.
Robin flies.
Ribbon ties.
Rabbit hops.
Rainbow arc.

A tub is a bath,
A cab is a taxi,
A cub is a baby,
A fib is a lie,
A sob is a cry,
A bob is a hair cut.
A hob is a cooker,
A crib is a cradle,
A crab is a crustacean....

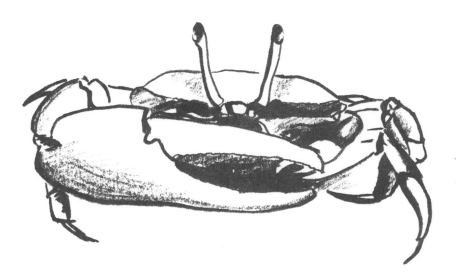

Blue sky, blaze of light.
Bleak night, black as coal.

Tumbler for a long drink.
Cobbler to make shoes.
Rambler walks for miles.
Gambler plays to win.

Ablution is washing oneself,
Oblong is a shape.
Oblique is at an angle,
Oblivion is having been forgotten.
Obliterate is to completely blot out.

Bulb hangs from the wire in the ceiling,
Bulb burns bright with electric brilliance.

Bulb deep down in the damp brown earth,
Bulb bursts into life once Spring arrives.

/br/ initial position

Brown bread, so we are told,
Brim full of health,
Brings bright eyes,
Breath fresh, and
Brilliant brain.
Brown bread,
Brown sugar,
Brown rice,
Brown earth,
What a brown world!

/br/ medial position

Abrupt - sudden.
Abbreviate - shorten.
Abridge - condense.
Abroad - overseas.

/rb/ final position
/r/ may be heard, or blend into vowel.

Child stands at curb;
Don't disturb or perturb
By going 'burb, burb, burb'

Ten little toes go out together,
Out together in the windy weather
Ten little toes in shoes of leather.
Ten little toes by the fireside stay.
Ten little toes in slippers gay,
Ten little toes are warm all day.

Traditional

/t/ medial position

Bitter Butter

Betty Botter bought some butter.
But, she said, this butter's bitter.
If I put it in my batter,
It will make my batter bitter.
But a bit of better butter
Will make my batter better.
So she bought a bit of better butter,
Better than her bitter butter,
And she put it in her batter
And it made her batter better.
So 'twas better Betty Botter
Bought a bit of better butter.

Anon

/t/ final position

Rat-a-tat-tat! Who is that?
Only grandma's pussy-cat.
What do you want?
A pint of milk.
Where is your money? In my pocket.
Where is your pocket? I forgot it.
Oh, you silly pussy-cat!

An old London Street game

/tr/ initial position

Trains

Train treats are train track trips.
Trains tread tricky tracks,
Trains uphill tramp 'trug, trug, trug,'
Trains downhill triumphantly try to fly;
Trains, the trendy way to travel!

/tr/ medial position

Attractive contrast of colours
Contributes a treat to the eye;

A contract is binding; when broken,
Contrite excuses are not an attribute.

20

/rt/ final position
/r/ may be heard or blend into vowel.

Naughty elephants squirt
Water, and roll in the dirt.
They enjoy some fun and a flirt
But they are careful not to hurt.

/lt/ final position

Halt! Who goes there?
Bolt the door, scared.
Colt gallops round the field, afraid.
Jolt of thunder,
Volt of lightening
Felt the storm's full force.

/ft/ final position

Two small boys climbed into the loft,
The loft is the roof space at the top of their croft.
A shaft of sunshine lit up a strange craft,
A craft that looked very much like a raft.
'A raft!' they yelled, 'Will you help us lift?'
'You daft kids', said Dad, 'It's best left,
The soft water collects in a tank that can't drift,
That craft won't shift!'

21

Twelve twisting twits
All did the splits.
Twelve plus twelve is
Twenty four.
Twenty four twits
Sat up from the splits,
Twelve twisting twits!

Twice two is four,
Twice four is more.
Twenty plus twenty
Is plenty, so don't ask for more!

/tw/ medial position

Between the lines
Between the trees
Between the oceans
Between the seas
Between our toes we feel the sand.

Done In

Dad in bed,
Dog seems dead,
Desperate to do a dance down at the disco.
Day has dawned,
Dad is up,
Dog is determinedly by the door.
Din was dreadful down at the disco,
Dearly wish I'd done what Dad said,
Done a deal, and gone to bed.

/d/ medial position

Rudder to steer a boat,
Fodder to feed cattle,
Udder to give milk,
Larder to keep food cool,
Ladder to climb up,
Adder to slip away from.

/d/ final position

Bad day, feel sad.
Good day, feel glad.
Cross day, feel mad.
Cold day, feel like food.
Wet day, wear my hood.
Hot day, happy mood.

Drip, drop,
Down the drain,
Drizzle, then
Drowning, drenching RAIN!

Address the envelope, gallop to the post,
Adrenaline pumping, full of hope; letter
Adrift in the big wide world, for the
Adroit postal service to deliver on time.

Dwell in a house,
Dwindle in size,
Dwarf is small.

Toddler is a fiddler,
Fiddles with anything.
Toddler is a muddler,
Muddles up everything.
Toddler is a paddler,
Paddles into puddles.
Toddler is a cuddler,
Cuddles up tight.

/ld/ final position

There once was a mouse
Who lived in a house,
A cold, cold house by the sea.
If I were a mouse
In that cold, cold house,
What a cold, cold mouse
I would be!

Traditional

Attishoo! Told you so, you've got a cold.
On the beach: Build a castle made of gold.
Car boot sale: Bold move, it's all sold!
Away too long: Unfold the cheese to find mould!

/rd/ final position
/r/ may be heard, or blend into vowel.

One, two, three,
First, second, third.
Third is three,
Three birds in a tree.
The third bird flew,
Leaving only two.

Call of Spring

Catkins catch the eye,
Catkins call the Spring,
Catkins canter and kick,
Catkins in the wind.
Catkins catch the eye,
Catkins cascading, cartwheeling,
Catkins call of Spring.

/c/ or /k/ medial position

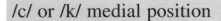

Pins and Things

A packet of pins
A racket of tins
A locket to wear
A jacket to tear
A bucket to kick
A ticket to clip
A wicket to fall
A cuckoo to call.

© Winslow Press 'k' 'g' kit

26

/ck/ or /k/ final position

Back before Dark

Quick! It will soon be dark!
Pack a rucksack, take a cake,
Pick up a sock, choc bar to suck,
Make for the door at the back,
Take the track that leads to the lake,
Look for the lake, and then the duck.
Duck goes 'Quack, quack, quack.'
Luck is in, see the chick,
Chick with the damaged beak!
Chuck in the cake, peck, peck, peck,
'Squeak, squeak, squeak,' the chick calls back,
'Look, I'll make it into a duck!'
Black thoughts of hungry, weak little chick,
Stuck in the mind, but now a cheerful spark.
Back home at a walk, happy, no need to talk.
Thick door opens without a creak,
Peek at the clock, pick up a book,
Back to finish homework, outside it's dark!

/cl/ initial position

The Fair

Clip clop clip clop
We're going to the fair
Clip clop clip clop
Clean ribbons in our hair

Clip clop clip clop
The clouds are bringing rain
Clip clop clip clop
We're going home again.

Traditional

/cl/ medial position

Reclaim the title,
Proclaim a victory.
Acclaim the winner,
Incline the head.
Recline in warmth,
Include everyone.
Decline to comment,
Acclimatize slowly.

/lk/ final position
/l/ is usually heard, but not in /walk/ /talk/.

The Incredible Hulk
Went into a sulk.
His great big bulk
Needed a good walk and a talk.
Instead he got a drink of milk,
And sat in a chair as soft as silk.

/cr/ initial position
/chr/ sounds as /cr/.

Cruel Christmas
Crumpets and crackers,
Crisps and cream cakes,
Crammed corners, crinkled crepe,
Crack, crunch, crazy crescendo...
Crowds at Christmas.

There was a crooked man
And he walked a crooked mile
He found a crooked sixpence
Beneath a crooked stile
He bought a crooked cat
Which caught a crooked mouse
And they all lived together
In a little crooked house.

Old Nursery Rhyme

/cr/ medial position

Knitting

Increase, decrease,
Knit another row.
Decrease, increase,
Incredible how knitting will grow.

Decrease, increase,
Now its nearly done.
Increase, decrease,
Incredible how knitting is fun!

© *Winslow Press 'k' 'g' kit*

/rk/ final position
/r/ may be heard or blend into vowel.

Channel Islands of Jersey, Guernsey, Alderney, Sark and Herm

On the Island of Sark
You feel free as a lark;
No cars leave their mark
Only a horse drawn cart to park;
Nothing moves far after dark
No worries on the island of Sark.

/qu/ initial position
/qu/ sounds aloud as /k/ + /w/ except at * where it is just /k/ + vowel.

Quickly, quickly,
Very quickly,
Runs the little mouse.
Quickly, quickly,
Very quickly,
Round about the house.

A follow-on verse comparing 'quickly' with the 'mouse', and 'slowly' like the 'snail' is on Page 50, /sl/ initial position.

Quiz Question
'Why does the Queen request the *queue to keep quiet?'
Answer
'Because "Q" was looking for "U".'

*Quay to walk along.
Quaint little village,
Quack on the duck pond.
Queer little alleyways,
Quick to explore.
Quarter the size of our town back home!

/qu/ medial position

Enquire about a job.
Require an exam.
Acquainted with knowledge.
Acquit myself better.
Request an interview.
Acquire the job!

Guess the Game

GO!
Getting going,
Galloping, galloping,
Got gap,
Gasping, gaining,
GOAL!
Goals galore,
Good game!

/g/ medial position

Luggage means travel.
Baggage means heavy bags.
Rigger means oil rig worker.
Rugger means tough sport.
Mugger means a menace.
Lugger means a small ship.
Regatta means boats racing.
Regular means even, steady.
Ragged means broken.
Jagged means uneven.
Regard means you've looked on /g/ for long enough!

Dog gives a wag,
Jumps on the rug,
Snug as a bug.
By comes a pig,
Dancing a jig,
Dog leaps at pig.
Pig lands on rug,
Tug goes dog,
Rug turns into game of tag.

/gl/ initial position

Glass tinkles,
Glass glows,
Glass gleams,
Glass glistens.

Glare of search lights.
Glacier cold.
Glaze hard gloss.
Glide of a snake.
Glade of green grass.
Glad to be happy.
Gloves for warmth.
Glow from heat.

Green grass
Grows gradually.
Greedy animals
Graze gratefully.

Grand day, dress up for
Grandad's birthday.
Grandma groans 'We're getting old'
Group gradually gathers,
Greeting each other graciously,
Great to be together, now let's
Grab some grub!

/gr/ medial position

The Bird

Hungry, hungry little bird,
Now you regret the Summer's gone.
Migrate, migrate little bird,
Get ready now, your journey's long.

33

/f/ initial position   voiceless fricative   *top teeth lightly on bottom lip*

Four fine feathered fowl
Faced forwards on a fence.

Extended, harder version is given on page 42.

Extended, harder version is given on page 42.

Felix cat
Met Fearless fox.
'Felix' said fox,
'Let's fool Farmer Ford
By finding a field,
And play for fun.'

Extended, harder version is given on page 42.

/f/ medial position

Huffing and puffing,
Laughing and coughing,
Sniffing and snuffling.

/f/ final position
/gh/ sounds as /f/.

Muff and Puff,
Two balls of fluff,
Huff and scuff,
Laugh and cough,
Sniff and snuff,
Enough, enough.

/f/ /fl/ and /fr/ initially

Farmer flings fruitful seed
Far upon furrowed field.

Paul King (Rudolf Steiner School)

/fl/ initial position

Flags

Flags fly,
Flags flutter,
Flags flap,
Flags flop,
When the wind falls.

/fl/ medial position

Affluent is rich;
Affliction is suffering.
Conflict is opposites;
Deflate is to empty of air.
Deflect is to turn aside;
Reflect is to throw back an image.
Reflex is automatic action.

/lf/ final position

In the Toy Shop

Rolf sat on the shelf.
Shelf also had an elf,
Elf called Alf.
Alf said to Rolf,
'Rolf, you are a handsome wolf.'
Wolf said to elf,
'Alf, lets play golf!'
'Golf?' said Alf,
Self-centred wolf can play golf by himself!

/fr/ initial position

Frog Fred

Fred is frightful,
Frightful Fred.
Fred is a frog.
Frog Fred jumped....
From....
Freedom onto my foot! Fearful,
Frightening Fred!

/fr/ medial position

Africa

Africa!
Africa's wild life is unique,
Refreshingly different, yet
Afraid to confront visitors with:
'Refrain from infringing on it'.

/rf/ final position
/r/ may be heard or take the vowel sound + /f/.

Try to surf on a scarf -
You'll be in for a laugh!

Vans

Vans dash,
Vans splash,
Vans come,
Vans go.

Vans are vital, carrying
Vast quantities of
Variable items:
Villager's alternative to the Heavy Goods
Vehicle!

Vans dash,
Vans splash,
Vans receive, and
Very soon deliver.

/v/ medial position

Fun Fair

Revolving big wheel at the Fun Fair,
Surviving death-defying Dodgem cars,
Reviving pink candy floss to munch,
Division of opinion: what to try next?

/v/ final position

Dive

Dive into water,
Dive deep down below,
Dive to where the fishes go.

Sky dive.
Car drive.
Disco rave.
Chocolate crave.
Starving save.
Kitchen slave.
Bee hive,
Bees alive!

/lv/ final position

Salve a bicycle wheel from the scrap heap,
Valve is all that needs replacing.

/th/ initial position   voiced fricative   *tongue tip between teeth, gently*

These are these,
And those are those.
But those are these,
And these are those,
As soon as we change places.

Traditional

/th/ initial position   voiceless fricative   *tongue tip between teeth, gently*

Thumbs we have one on each hand.
Thimbles won't fit on our thumbs.
Think of number thirty - 30 -
Thirty pence in my purse,
Thin purse until Mum came in,
Thank you! A lovely shiny pound.

/thr/ initial position
/th/ always voiceless when followed by /r/.

Three little rabbits looked
Through the hedge.
Three little rabbits thought what a
Thrill to explore beyond.
Three little rabbits didn't see
Thread strung across their way.
Three little rabbits tripped up that day!

/th/ medial position
Always voiced.

Weather

Whether the weather be fine,
Or whether the weather be not,
Whether the weather be cold,
Or whether the weather be hot,
We'll weather the weather,
Whatever the weather,
Whether we like it or not!

Anon

/th/ final position
Voiceless except when 'with' is used.

Moth goes North.
Moth goes South.
Moth lands on a path.
Moth lies on a warm table cloth
Moth stops us both.
Moth so lovely we hold our breath.

/th/ /f/ and /v/ sounds mixed

Fingers and thumbs, fingers and thumbs,
Ten fine fellows to help with our sums.
Five on the left, and five on the right,
Working together we'll get the sums right.

Paul King. Paul suggests finger and left/right exercises with the poem.

41

One, Two, Three, Four, Five, Six, Seven, Eight, Nine, Ten....

Eleventh, twelfth, thirteenth, fourteenth, fifteenth....

Monday, Tuesday, Wednesday, Thursday, Friday, Saturday, Sunday.

I saw a fish in a fountain pool.
With fins as thin as a filigree fan.

Paul King

Felix the cat met Fearless the fox.
'Felix', said the fox.
'Let's fool the farmer by finding a field
And playing there fearlessly.'

'Thanks' said the cat, but then added
'I fear that would be that.'
'Bother,' thought Fearless,
'Felix is too clever for an old game like that'

Four fine feathered friends
Faced front upon a fence.

Four fine feathered friends
Flew in a flash to freedom.

Paul King

Sea Side

Sun,
Sea,
Sand,
Sailing boat,
Sandcastle,
Seagulls,
Seaweed,
Summer holiday....
Salty,
Satisfying,
Super!

/s/ medial position
Sometimes /s/ - as in 'position' - sounds as /z/. Sound /s/ often spelt /ce/ or /ss/.

An Announcement:

'Would it be possible for the passenger named Passmore to take a message from a person called Wilson - crossing through Bristol to Glasgow - who will be waiting in the passage by Parcel Reception?'

43

This is a piece of 'prose', or 'sentences':

Once upon a time a big red bus went out alone, without the boss who was the driver and the conductor all in one. The big red bus went down the road; it went by a horse who was eating grass; it went by a house where a mouse lived; and the big red bus went on by a class of children who were out walking back from the games field with their teacher.

'Please give us a lift' they all said together, 'Please! Please! Please!'

Big red bus could not pass this class of children, as he knew they would be cross. 'Jump in, I will make sure you get back to base without having to chase.' The children were happy, and red bus was happy when they all gave him a big kiss. Then he went on to his bus base, and gave the boss a purse with all the children's fare money in it; even the boss forgot to be cross with the big red bus!

/sp/ initial position

Spiders spin speedily,
Spin, spiders, spin
Sparkling spider's web!

Spider, spider,
What are you spinning?
A cloak for a fairy
I'm now beginning.

Spin, spider, spin,
Now that you're spinning
A cloak for a fairy
With all the trimming.

Nursery Rhyme - adapted to keep /sp/ but no additional /s/ blends

44

Inspired to DO something - perhaps an
Expedition, or an exploration, become an
Expert in rock climbing or caving
Inspect the deep sea bed, or help build
Respect for our environment, dispel all
Despair with responsible actions, even
Aspire to new heights, without the need for an
Aspirin to save perspiration turning into expiration!

/sp/ final position

In flew a wasp
When I was eating a crisp,
My jaws I did clasp
Now I talk with a lisp!

/st/ initial position

Stamp on stick - crack.
Steam from kettle - hiss.
Stone touching stone - click.

Stop! Stand still!
Look right, left, right.
Stop and stare,
Before you
Step -
Into that road.

Stairs

Stairs go steeply up,
Stairs come staggering down,
Steep stairs,
Steady stairs,
Stairs,
        Stairs,
                Stairs !

Mister Blister
Had a sister,
Her name was
Sister Plaster!

Catastrophe

Master of the
Coaster tried to avert
Disaster by
Instructing: 'Avoid
Destruction, go
Faster, use a
Booster, turn on the
Toaster, let's
Bluster our way out of this
Blistering day!

/st/ final position

First

Fast past the post,
FIRST!
Must not boast
That I'm the best!

Last

Toast has a crust;
I like toast,
But I leave the crust.
Why must I be last?
Always asked to eat the crust!

Ghost

I saw a ghost,
Eating toast,
Half way up
The lamp post!

Traditional

Mr East gave a feast.
Mr West was the guest.
Mr North came last.
Mr South ate enough to burst.

Adapted Traditional Rhyme

47

Skating

Scarf around neck,
Skates are on,
Skating over ice,
Skirting the edge,
Skimming the surface,
Skating skilfully along.

Skipping

Skipping is fun,
Skipping is fun,
Skipping is fun for everyone!

The longer you skip,
The better you skip,
So skip, skip, skip!

Traditional Rhyme

/sc/ or /sk/ medial position

Tosca and Whisky

Tosca was a cat with one whisker.
Whisky was a dog who was frisky.
Whisky chased Tosca,
Tosca went like a bullet from a musket.
Whisking round a turn that was risky,
Tosca leapt home to her basket.
Whisky came briskly in time for a biscuit.

48

/sc/ or /sk/ final position

The elephant with one tusk
Charged the gunman at dusk;
The gunman's task
Was not to stand and ask,
So he took no risk
His departure was brisk!

/scr/ initial position

Scrumptious

Scrumping apples, oh, what fun!
Scramble, scrum,
Scrape, screech,
Scratch, scream,
Scrumping apples not always fun!

/sm/ initial position

Small boy grows into
Smart guy grows into
Smash hit grows into BIG
SMILE!

Small smoke smoulders,
Hot fire flames.

Smile after praise,
Cry after smack.

/sn/ initial position

Snow falls
Snow flakes
Snow balls
Snowmen
Snow is such fun!

/sl/ initial position

Slip and slide,
Slowly down the slope.
Sleighs and sledges,
Slither on the slant.

Slowly, slowly,
Very slowly,
Creeps the garden snail.
Slowly, slowly,
Very slowly,
Up the wooden pail.

Traditional

A first verse comparing 'quickly' with the 'mouse' and 'slowly' like the 'snail' is on page 30, /qu/ initial position.

/sw/ initial position

Swing me over the water,
Swing me over the sea,
Swing me over the garden wall,
And swing me home for tea.

Traditional Rhyme

Swan swam over the sea,
Swim, swan, swim!
Swan swam back again,
Well swum swan!

Traditional Rhyme

/spr/ initial position

Spring Time

Spring has sprung,
Spread our wings.
Sprays of flowers,
Sprinkling showers.

/str/ initial position

Stray Moment

Strand of straw
Blows down straight street.
Stray cat strolls
Towards the straw,
Strokes it with his paw.
Strand of straw stirs,
Stray cat and strand of straw
Strike up a good game!

Squirrel

Squeak, squeak,
Squawk, squawk,
Squirrel squares to the world.
Squeezes nuts open,
Squanders empty shells everywhere.

/spl/ initial position

Splash!
Splish, Splash, Splosh,
Splitter, splat, splot.
What a splishy, splashy, splendidly sploshy puddle!

Fifth of November

Splendidly clear is the night
Splendour of fireworks break the sky.
Splattering dashes of colour bright
Splashes of light and sound upward fly.

Splutter of bonfires, burning heat,
Splinters and sparks darting carelessly,
Splitting groups of people, who shuffle their feet,
Splurging once a year outside, burning Guy Fawkes fearlessly.

voiced fricative   *tongue and alveolar ridge close, teeth very close*

Italian Sweet

Zip, zap, zany Zabaglione.

/z/ initial and medial positions

Zig, zag, Zebra's stripes,
Zing dizzily,
Dazing grazing cows!

/z/ medial and final positions
Spelt with /s/ or /z/.

Pisa

The Tower of Pisa
Is a bit of a teaser.
Call it lazy,
Or even crazy.
The Tower of Pisa
Leans further and further,
As the years go by.

/z/ final position

Bees Buzz

Buzz, buzz, buzz,
Buzy little bee.
Buzz where you like,
But don't sting me!

Traditional

/x/ medial position
short /e/ + /k/ + /s/ sounds.

Exact, Extra, Extraordinary, Extinct
All shows up on the X-Ray !

/x/ final position
Said as /k/ + /s/ sounds; sometimes spelt /cks/ at ends of words.

Mr Fox
Knits pairs of socks
Whilst he's got the chicken pox.
Mr Fox
Lives in a house shaped like a box,
Built of bricks and sticks,
Which he tightly locks
When he goes out with Mrs Fox.

First Day of Junior School

Ship shape,
Shoes shine,
Shuffling shyly;
Shock of the sudden
Shake of the new school bell.

Shades of laughter,
Shapes of friends,
Shining sun,
Shadows sharp;
Shed those shivers,
Shout and sing -
Sure way to share the fun!

/sh/ medial position

Yuk

Mushy peas,
Slushy snow,
Splashy paint,
Crashing thunder,
Rushing people,
Clashing music,
Washing dishes,
Wishing them all away!

/sh/ final position

Rush, must dash!
Dash as bell rings 'finish'.
Push against the crush.
Hush, time to play hide-and-seek round the bush,
Wish, oh wish at the end of each day we didn't have to wash!

/shr/ initial position

Shrill shriek from the shrub as the
Shrewd shrike shot its bill into the
Shrinking shrew.

/zh/ medial position   voiced fricative   *tongue edges and upper side teeth very close*

Measure the hours -
Leisure means pleasure -
Pleasure cannot be measured.

'H' for Hospital

Head held high,
Heart hitting hard,
Hat held in hand,
'H' sign hovers.
Hospital Reception here I am again!
Horrors, help, hopefully....
Happily huffing past the 'H' sign.
Home, home sweet home again!

/h/ medial position

'Ahoy!'

Ahoy there! Ahoy!
Ahead! Behind!
Ahoy! Boat ahead.
Ahoy! Boat behind.
Ahoy! We have not rehearsed.
Ahoy! We are sinking ahead.
Ahoy! We are sinking behind.
Ah...arrr
     rr
       rr....

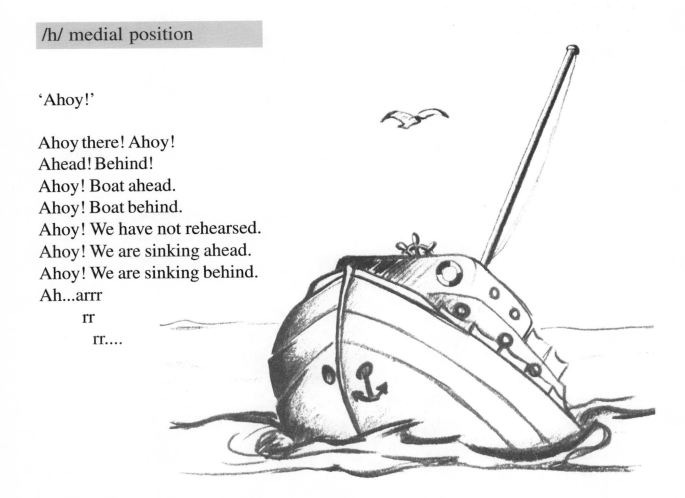

Chop, chop, chipperty chop,
Chop off the bottom, and chop off the top.

What there is left we will pop in the pot,
Chop, chop, chipperty chop!

Traditional

/ch/ medial position

Snatches

Hutches for tame rabbits;
Watches to tell the time;
Witches fly high on their broomsticks;
Stitches make mischief by coming undone;
Catches on the cricket pitches;
Achieving goals, well done.

/ch/ final position

Check your watch,
Strike a match,
Lift the latch,
Feel your breath catch!

Which switch is the switch, Miss, for Ipswich?
It's the Ipswich switch which I require,
You've switched my switch on Southwich
Which is quite the wrong wire,
So please could you switch my switch to Ipswich,
As it's the Ipswich switch that I require.

Traditional

Jolly Jug

Jack jumped over the jug.
Jug jittered,
Jug juddered,
Jug jingled,
Just in jest!

/j/ medial position

Original masterpieces -
Aboriginal art.
Rejecting the dark age -
Rejoicing in the dawn.
Legends on stone -
Subjects clearly drawn.
Legions of years ago -
Objects of wonder.

/j/ final position

Day at the Zoo

Lion in a cage
Roars with rage.

Boy nears ledge
Falls over edge.

Lion in a cage stops his trudge
In a flash forgets his grudge.

Boy never has time to budge
All that's left is a metal badge!

/l/ initial position | voiced lateral non-fricative | *tongue tip touching centre of alveolar ridge*

Lambs leap,
Ladies laugh,
Lads lie,
Leopards laze.

/l/ initial and medial positions

We like to lick lollipops,
Lovely coloured lollipops;
I like yellow lollipops,
You like red lollipops;
Lovely flavoured lollipops.

/l/ medial position

Silver cup for sailing;
Gold medallion for golfing.

Ducks Ditty

All along the backwater,
Through the rushes tall,
Ducks are a-dabbling,
Up tails all!

Duck's tails, drakes' tails,
Yellow feet a-quiver,
Yellow bills all out of sight,
Busy in the river!

Slushy green undergrowth
Where the roach swim -
Here we keep our larder,
Cool and full and dim.

Every one for what he likes!
We like to be
Heads down, tails up,
Dabbling free!

High in the blue above
Swifts whirl and call -
We are down a-dabbling
Up tails all!

Kenneth Grahame (1859-1932)

/l/ with consonant blends in final position

/pl/

People climb the steeple -
Steeple will topple,
Topple and buckle,
Buckle and ruckle,
Ruckle and ripple,
Ripple and tipple,
Tipple and crash down among all the people.

/bl/

Bubble, bubble, toil and trouble.

Rumble of thunder.
Tumble of rain.
Terrible flooding.
Sensible to play 'Scrabble' inside.

Wibble wobble, wibble wobble, jelly on a plate.
Wibble wobble, wibble wobble, jelly in a state.

/tl/
When /tl/ is prefixed with /s/ the sound becomes /sl/.

Rattle of battle
Rustle of cattle
Bustle of a beetle
Hustle of being little.

/dl/

Bridle and saddle, bridle and saddle,
Horses dress with a bridle and saddle.

/cl/

No longer a tricycle,
But a practical bicycle,
Shines with a twinkle,
Through traffic in a pickle,
A bicycle is never fickle.

/gl/

Tangle of hair -
Struggle to brush,
Bangle to wear -
Triangle of colour for a dress,
Single shoe - now where's the other?
Giggle happily, out with Mother.

/fl/

Trifle with a rifle -
Rifle will stifle,
Stifle will baffle,
Baffle makes kerfuffle.
Kerfuffle is dreadful -
Dreadful to be fearful,
Fearful of a rifle,
Rifle that can stifle.

/sl/
/stl/ spelling said as /sl/.

Hustle and bustle,
Bustle at the castle.
Castle in a hassle,
Hassle over a whistle -
Whistle found under a thistle.

/zl/

Teazle the Weasel
Has a puzzle.
He must wear a muzzle
When out on the razzle,
In case his teeth dazzle.
Teazle the Weasel
Out in a muzzle...
But that's the puzzle:
How can he guzzle
When wearing a muzzle?

One windy Wednesday morning,
Whistling at the window,
The window cleaner
Washed and wiped
Whoosh — whoosh —
Whistle, whistle,
All at my window!

Claire Nash-Wortham

Warm are the winds in the woodlands,
Wafting their way through the leaves,
Weaving and winding and whispering,
Like wind flowing over the sheaves.

Warm is the water in summer,
Wafting its way to my feet,
Watery, watery wavelets,
Like wind flowing over the wheat.

Rev Charles Kingsley (1819-1875)

/w/ medial position

The award
Is a reward,
For sewing
The sail which broke away,
And was flapping hard when we awoke,
To find the yacht all awash.
Yet no-one was a coward.

/w/ final position

How now brown cow,
Why do you look so sad?
Down on the grassy ground I found you,
Grazing with crowds of cows around you.
How now brown cow,
Why do you look so sad?

Traditional

/wh / initial position
Spelt /wh/ and usually said as /w/ except 'whose' and 'who' said as /h/ + vowel.

Whizz goes the car,
Whack goes an arm,
Wham goes a fist,
Whistle goes the Referee,
Whoopee, this is great to see!

Where are we going?
What will we do?
Why must we wait?
When we're longing to start?
Which way will we travel?
Whose best friend shall we take?
Who could guess what a lot of questions we ask!

Yellow sun,
Yellow yolk,
Yellow custard,
Yellow coat.

On the Menu

Yabby, yabby, yaffle, yolk,
Yam, yarrow, yapock, yoghurt,
Yeast, yucca, yum-yum,
Yes, you can eat all of them!

Yesterday ... a yearling, a youngster, youthful.

Rain

Rain runs in rivulets,
Rushing to the river,
Racing like a regatta,
Rising to the rim.

/r/ initial and medial positions

I am the rider of the wind,
The stirrer of the storm;
The hurricane I left behind
Is yet with lightening warm.

George Gordon Byron (1788-1824)

/r/ medial position

I will borrow the barrow to carry the berries.
Tomorrow, I will borrow the barrow to carry the marrows.
The day after tomorrow, I will borrow the barrow to carry the carrots.
Yesterday, I borrowed a lorry to carry the parrots from the ferry.
The day before yesterday, I arranged my programme for the week!

/r/ final position
Usually takes a vowel quality in speech.

Purr, purr,
Cat with fur,
Lives with mother,
Father, sister, brother.

Mighty mountains
Make mortal men
Mere morsels.

/m/ medial position

Swimming

Rumble, tumble,
Summer swimmer,
Skimming and humming,
As the waves hammer,
Then coming to calmer water.

/m/ final position

Rum, tum, tum,
Rum, tum, tum,
Tiddly-om-pom, pom,
Tiddly-om-pom, pom
Went the drum.

Traditional

Nodding off,
Night nestles,
Nocturnal noises near,
Naughtily playing on
Nervous imagination.

/n/ medial position

Monday morning....
Raining....
Planning....
Running....
Cunning....

/n/ final position

Fun Run?

Skin on bone;
Pain in vain.
Never run again....
In London Marathon.

Sums

Add, plus = addition
Take, minus = subtraction
Divide, into = division
Multiply, times = multiplication

Attention!

What a commotion!
Train didn't stop at the station!
People throw away caution,
They demand attention,
'Missed meeting a relation,
Waiting in expectation.'
Demand a new connection,
Make immediate application,
For a full investigation;
They make a sensation,
In the newspaper's local edition,
What is the reaction?
No real satisfaction -
For there's no long lasting implication,
In the train's unusual action,
It's over, it's past, it's on to the next attraction!

'Celebrating'

Ringing bells.
Singing voices.
Laughing children
Longing for dawning
Of Christmas morning!

Merrily, merrily, ring the bells!
Ding-dong, ding-dong, ding-dong, ding-dong,
Chiming and rhyming their musical swells!
Ding-dong, ding-dong, ding-dong, ding-dong,
Singing and ringing they tunefully call!
Ding-dong, ding-dong, ding-dong, ding-dong,
Tidings, good tidings we bring to you all!
Ding-dong, ding-dong, ding-dong, ding-dong!

Miss Anne H McAllister

VOWELS

These are 23 of the most commonly used vowel sounds. Accents or dialects in spoken English add to the variations. Vowels are always made with a free flow of voiced air passing through the open, variously-shaped mouth.

Pure short vowels

/a/   *front of mouth, lips well apart*

Fat cat
Sat on the mat,
And spat
At the rat,
The rat,
The rat.

/e/   *front of mouth, lips spread apart*

Red bed
Sent to the shed,
Fed up bed
Without a leg,
A leg,
A leg.

/i/   *front of mouth, lips slightly spread apart*

Thin tin pin
Thin pin twinkles
In the bin,
The bin,
The bin.

/o/   *back of mouth, lips rounded, well open*

Hoppy frog
On and off the log,
Not stopping for long
On the top of the log,
The log,
The log.

/u/ *centre of mouth, lips well open neutrally*

Up, umbrella, up,
And I'll keep under,
Under,
Under.

/oo/ *back of mouth, lips well rounded apart*

Look, look, a book,
A book on a hook.
A hook, look,
A book hook!

/er/ *centre of mouth, lips apart neutrally*

Mother, father, brother, sister,
Over-joyed to see each other.

Pure long vowels

/ee/ *front of mouth, lips spread back apart*

We see a bee
Flee from heat
To the sea,
The sea,
The sea.

/ah/ *back of mouth, well open with neutral lips*

Car goes far, far, far
On roads of tar, tar, tar.

/aw/ *back of mouth, lips apart, somewhat rounded*

Poor sore paw,
Caught between floor and door,
Floor and door.

/oo/ *back of mouth, lips rounded closely, yet apart*

Soon, soon,
Looming,
A boom on the moon,
The moon,
The moon.

/er/ *centre of mouth, lips apart neutrally*

Bird heard a word,
In a world of words,
Bird learnt a word, a word.

Diphthongs *Slide sound, tongue and jaw moves, lips apart.*
Two vowels heard, emphasis on first sound.

/ay/

Hooray,
Today we make hay,
Without delay we make hay,
Make hay.

/oh/

Mow, grow. Grow, mow.
Sow a row,
Hoe a row,
Grow, mow, grow.

/I/

I ride high,
High like a kite
Into the sky,
The sky,
The sky.

/ow/

How now, brown cow,
Brown cow, brown cow.
Down on the ground I found you,
Browsing with crowds of cows around you.
How now, brown cow,
Brown cow, brown cow.

Traditional

/oi/

Boy with a toy,
What joy,
Joy,
Joy.

/eer/

Year in, year out,
Cheer in, clear out;
New Year is near,
Is near,
Is near.

/air/

There in the air
The Great Bear,
The Bear,
The Bear.

/ure/

Endure a cure
To be pure,
Pure,
Pure.

/ew/

Few of you mew,
Mew like a kitten that's new,
Or dance on the dew,
The dew,
The dew.

Triphthongs   *three distinct vowel sounds, emphasis on first*

/ire/

'Iron on fire',
Dire trouble
Or a liar
A liar,
A liar?

/our/

Our flowers
Need showers,
Showers,
Showers.

77

APPENDIX

PARENT - ORIENTATED BOOKS

POETRY BOOKS FOR YOUNGER CHILDREN (with good big print)

Animals Like Us	Puffin Books	(ed) A Bradman
A Mouse in my Roof	Puffin Books	R Edwards
Poems for 7 and Under	Puffin Books	R and N Edwards
Poems for 9 and Under	Puffin Books	R and N Edwards
Poems for over 10 years old	Puffin Books	R and N Edwards
Early in the Morning	Puffin Books	Charles Causley
A Picnic of Poetry	Puffin Books	(ed) A Harvey
Quick Let's Get Out of Here	Puffin Books	M Rosenand, Q Blake
Laughter is an Egg	Puffin Books	J Agard
Silly Verse for Kids	Puffin Books	Spike Milligan
Heard it in the Playground	Puffin Books	Allan Ahlberg
The Jolly Postman	Puffin Books	Allan Ahlberg
The Jolly Christmas Postman	Puffin Books	Allan Ahlberg
The Mighty Slide	Puffin Books	Allan Ahlberg
(Also some 50 other titles)	Puffin Books	Allan Ahlberg
Rhyme Stew	Puffin Books	Roald Dahl
Revolting Rhymes	Puffin Books	Roald Dahl
An Imaginary Menagerie	Puffin Books	Roger McGough
Sky in the Pie	Puffin Books	Roger McGough
Helen Highwater	Puffin Books	Roger McGough
Nailing the Shadow	Puffin Books	Roger McGough
I Like This Poem	Puffin Original	(ed) K Webb
Whiskers and Rhymes	Walker Books	Arnold Lobel

RHYMING PICTURE BOOKS

Each Peach Pear Plum	Picture Puffin	J and A Ahlberg
Hairy Macleary from Donaldsais Dairy	Picture Puffin	L Dodd

COUNTING BOOKS IN RHYME

Hippos Go Berserk	Little Mammoth	S Boynton
1, 2, 3, and Things	MacMillan	C McNaughton

RHYME AND ALLITERATION

Hairy Bear	Nelson	Story Chest
Nutshell Library	Collins	M Sendak

ALLITERATIVE BOOKS

Animalia	Picture Puffin	G Base
C is for Clown	Collins	S and J Berenstin
Dr. Seuss's ABC	Collins	
A Prize for Percival	Picture Puffin	A Langoulant

TEACHER - ORIENTATED BOOKS

CONNECTED TO SPEECH

Speech Rhymes	A & C Black	Clive Sansom
Acting Rhymes	A & C Black	Clive Sansom
Counting Rhymes	A & C Black	Clive Sansom
Rhyme Rhymes	A & C Black	Clive Sansom
Ideal Voice and Speech Training	Samuel French	K Parkin
Anthology of British Tongue-Twisters	Samuel French	K Parkin
Clear Speech	A & C Black	M Morrison
Speech Exercise for Juniors and Seniors	L.A.M.D.A.	Jeffrey Du Cann Grenfell-Hill
Tongue and Lip Exercises	L.A.M.D.A.	Jeffrey Du Cann Grenfell-Hill

PHONICS

The Phonics Handbook	Jolly Learning	Sue Lloyd
Cued Articulation	Acer/Stass	Jane Passy
Cued Vowels	Acer/Stass	Jane Passy

PHONETICS

Practical Phonetics	Pitman	J Wells & G Colson
Simple Phonetics for Teachers	Methuen	J Smith & M Bloor

PRACTICAL SPEECH AND LANGUAGE

Anthology of Verse and Prose	L.A.M.D.A.	LAMDA Examination
Choral Speaking	L.A.M.D.A.	Marjorie Emery
Talking Points	Stass	
Specific Learning Difficulties (Dyslexia) - A Teacher's Guide		Margaret Crombie
Working with Children's Language	Winslow Press	J Cooke, D William
Speech and Language Catalogue	Winslow Press	

ADDRESSES

LAMDA London Academy of Music and Dramatic Art
(Examinations Board) Tower House 226 Cromwell Road LONDON SW5 0SR

Winslow Press Telford Road BICESTER Oxon OX6 0TS (Child Development Catalogue available)

Stass Publications 44 North Road Ponteland Northumberland NE20 9UR

BY THE SAME AUTHOR

TAKE TIME   The Robinswood Press   M Nash-Wortham and J Hunt
(Movement exercises for parents, teachers and therapists of children with difficulties in speaking,
reading, writing and spelling.)